I0475122

Starting an Online Business 101

From the library of the
New Thrive Learning Institute

Published under Creative Commons License - NonCommercial-ShareAlike 3.0 Unported

Get Related Materials

from Our Free Library

Instant Access – Join Here

Click or type into your browser:

http://livesensical.com/go/byob/

LEGAL NOTICE:

The Publisher has strived to be as accurate and complete as possible in the creation of this report, notwithstanding the fact that he does not warrant or represent at any time that the contents within are accurate due to the rapidly changing nature of the Internet.

While all attempts have been made to verify information provided in this publication, the Publisher assumes no responsibility for errors, omissions, or contrary interpretation of the subject matter herein. Any perceived slights of specific persons, peoples, or organizations are unintentional.

In practical advice books, like anything else in life, there are no guarantees of income made. Readers are cautioned to reply on their own judgment about their individual circumstances to act accordingly.

This book is not intended for use as a source of legal, business, accounting or financial advice. All readers are advised to seek services of competent professionals in legal, business, accounting, and finance field.

Table of Contents

Introduction...1
Why Start An Online Business?..4
The Four Keys To Business Success.................................5
Before You Start...13
How to Set Up Your Business Plan.................................15
What Type of Business Is Best For You?.........................17
How to Set Up an Online Business.................................19
Affiliate Marketing Explained.......................................22
How To Marketing Your Online Business.......................27
Conclusion...30
Bonus...31

Introduction

When you're setting up an online business, you must treat it as just that – a business. You must be prepared to put in the time and effort to reap the rewards. You must be prepared to invest some capital. You do not need to put in large amounts of cash, but you do want to have some working capital.

The best place to begin is by picking what you like from the existing successful online business models already out there. Talk to others who have already made money in the niche that you have chosen, and then study their techniques, implement their strategies and become successful.

So what sort of business would you like to run? Some of the more popular types of online businesses are: selling goods at auction sites such as Ebay, creating and selling digital products and setting up websites for offline businesses. You may want to make downloadable audio and video products for your customers, or you may just want to get into affiliate marketing.

If you choose to set up an Ebay store:

- You have immediate access to millions of customers.

- You have the opportunity to sell anything from cars to collectibles

- Setting up an account on Ebay is straightforward, and the costs relating to auctioning items on this site are extremely low.

However, it is important that you familiarize yourself with the site. So take a look at the different categories and auctions that are already taking place. Also check out their "How to Sell" section on the site.

For some, the thought of creating their own products seems very daunting, but if you happen to be an expert in a particular niche, then coming up with ideas should not be that difficult. It is important that you carry out some market research to make sure that people would buy related items.

Make a note of what is selling well and formulate some questions that someone who is interested in this product might ask. Do an interview that answers all the questions you have come up with.

But if this just all seems too much, then why not get someone else to write some books for you? Think about hiring a ghostwriter. But this may be something to consider when you have a bit more money in the business account. So really, the next best way to make money with an online business is by selling someone else's products as an affiliate. As previously mentioned, we will look more closely at affiliate marketing in another chapter of this book.

Starting an Online Business 101 - 3

The best way of starting an online business is to do it in an area that you are knowledgeable or passionate about. This will help you to focus your attention, as well as help to create a small income more quickly. But over a period of time, you will soon develop new skills, and through persistence and perseverance, you will soon see some very good results appear.

Why Start An Online Business?

For many people, they decide to start an online business to earn an extra income. However, what starts as a part time venture, often becomes a full time career.

Another reason that people decide to start up an online business is that they have more control over their life. It provides them with a chance to spend more time with their family and friends. They no longer need to get up in the morning to rush off to work and get caught up in traffic. Now the time which would normally be wasted sitting in traffic can be used to their advantage. Plus, it is up to you when you work, so if you don't want to start until late in the morning, you do not need to.

Because of the rapid advance in technology, many online businesses tend to be prosperous. Low start up costs and overhead make it much simpler to generate a high Return On Investment (ROI) than in the offline world.

There is little or no need for mountains of paperwork and documents. What you really need to get an online business going is a computer, and a high speed Internet connection.

As you can see, setting up an online business might be the ideal choice for you.

The Four Keys To Business Success

Now that you know what pitfalls to avoid, you are ready to focus on the important aspects of ensuring your success. Even if your business has been around for years, getting back to the basics will help you pinpoint areas you have overlooked in the past, and help you build a stronger business for the future.

The four keys to your business success are:

1. Mindset

2. Focus

3. Education,

4. Action.

Mindset

The way you think, directly affects the results you get from your business. If you look at your business as a hobby, you will make a hobby income. If you treat your business as the professional entity that it is, your income will match your expectations. Although it may seem like psycho-babble, the way you think and view your business has a huge effect on whether you can actually buy your shiny yellow Corvette, or whether you can only afford the gas.

Starting an Online Business 101 - 6

Here's your new mindset: You are the President and CEO of your own company. It doesn't matter if you are the only person in your company, and your company consists of a 10-year-old computer sitting in the dusty corner of your bedroom. No one cares about your company except you. Your customers only care what your company can provide for them.

Next, take a realistic look at what you want to achieve. It's easy to see the success stories online and get caught up in the excitement. But look behind the scenes to see what actually happened to achieve those successes. There was a lot of groundwork that went into creating the results you read about. The money is there, but it takes some work to get to it.

To prove this point, we'll look at TheBusinessProfessional.com. One of the milestones in the company's history was generating $41,439 in sales in 17 days. But there's more to the story.

The Business Professional was born almost 2 years before the first major sales achievement. Originally, it was an online portal with a print quality magazine. Then it was transformed into a membership website.

The sales were generated, for the most part, by affiliates. The affiliates made a 50% commission, so $20,000 was paid to them. After payment processing fees, hosting and other miscellaneous fees, there was approximately $20,000 left to run the business and draw an income. So as Paul Harvey used to say, "Now you know the rest of the story."

So when you see stories of large amounts of money in short periods of time, keep in mind there is always a story behind the story. Remember to keep your expectations realistic.

Look at your business as if you were climbing a ladder. You have to lift your foot up to the first rung before you can reach the second rung. You have to make your first $10 sale before you make your first $100 sale. You have to experience your first $100 month before you have your first $500 month.

With perseverance and the right mindset, you can reach your goals, but you have to walk before you can run.

Focus

The next battle you're going to wage is with your mind. You need to stay focused on one task at a time. Pinpoint your focus to stay effective. When you sit at your computer, you are there to get a job done. There are hundreds of distractions online and offline, but you need to focus on the task at hand or your work will never get completed.

We all suffer from information overload. When you are online, it's easy to start out with great intentions of completing a task like answering email, and 2 hours later find yourself surfing mindlessly. You click on a link in an email that takes you to a website that leads you to another website with intriguing information in a link that... you get the picture. We've all been there. So you need to guard your focus and not lose sight of what you're actually supposed to be doing while you are sitting in front of your computer screen.

You have invested in this course to learn how to tap into the financial power of the Internet, so focus on the course and ignore everything else for the time being. You will build a solid business faster by keeping your focus.

To prove this point, look at the results of a recent experiment. Whether you agree or disagree with the methodology, the outcome is fascinating.

An experiment was conducted with a group of mentally challenged people. Each person had the ability to listen to simple instructions and carry out a simple task. None of them could do more than one simple task at a time, but all of them were able to complete menial tasks on a computer.

The top person in the group had been taught how to copy and paste text from a Word document into a simple form on a website. Each day, he would sit down at the computer for 20 minutes, copy and paste exactly as he'd been shown and then turn off the computer. This was his "job" every single day, day-in, day-out.

The text he was copying and pasting from the Word document into the form on the website was a simple article. He was given a new article each morning to copy into an article submission website and then push the send button. That was all he did. That was all he knew how to do. He didn't suffer from information overload. He simply followed the instructions he had been given. Each article promoted a website. After 3 weeks of sending out one article a day, the website made its' first sale, then another and another until the website was making at least one sale a day.

If a mentally challenged person can generate sales from a website, using one simple tactic, so can you. The key to making it happen is focus – your focus.

Narrow your focus and block out all the other noise in your life. Focus on this course until it is crystal clear and follow each step exactly as it's presented. Do not hop around, don't get side tracked, don't get bogged down with information. Follow the steps in the order they have been presented and you will have a solid business that you are proud of.

Education

Now that you have the proper mindset and you are focused, let's move into training mode. This is the third key to unlocking your business success. The course you are taking right now is your education. By the time you are finished this course, you'll know exactly how to set up, run and profit from your online business.

As you take your business to new levels of profitability, you want to keep learning and advancing. It's beneficial to read a business publication or listen to a business audio for at least half an hour each day. This way, you are continuing your education daily, but also working on your business. Educate yourself every day, but make sure you put your education into action. Don't get stuck in education mode and forget to act on your new knowledge.

Action

This is the vital key to success. You need to pare down your actions. Your only productive business actions are the ones that are helping to increase your business. The rest is wasting valuable action time. Surfing the Internet is not a productive action unless you are researching new opportunities. If you are researching, you need to limit your surfing to include only the subject matter that is essential to making decisions. It's very easy to get sidetracked and waste hours upon hours and getting nothing productive accomplished. You need to concentrate and stay focused.

Starting an Online Business 101 - 11

If you have a home based business, diligently set aside a block of time every single day that is your business time. No one should disturb you during that time. You have to discipline yourself to keep that time as business time.

Before you sit down at your computer, decide what you want to accomplish. If you want to write an autoresponder message and update your website with a new article, those are your priorities. Talking to your friends on Skype, and surfing for irrelevant information can be done after you have accomplished your goals.

If you are able to sit down at your computer undisturbed for several hours, break your time into blocks to ensure you maximize your effectiveness. The most important part of your business is your marketing. It should be the very first thing you do.

If you have 3 hours, your schedule could look like this:

Hour 1: Write and submit an article (marketing)

Hour 2: Edit a report (project development)

Hour 3: Answer email (administration)

Your daily actions will determine how successful your business is and how quickly you join the ranks of the high-level income earners. If you don't set up little mini plans for yourself, each time you sit down at the computer, you will easily waste your time and accomplish little or nothing.

Don't confuse activity with accomplishment.

Before You Start

Where to work from

Choose a location that is comfortable for you. You can work from home or you can rent an office. Some people find it easier to focus if they are in an office environment while others enjoy the freedom of multitasking at home. Right now as I write this, I'm also doing the laundry :)

How to market your business

Marketing is the key to a thriving business. Try everything online and offline. Read marketing books, take a basic marketing course and familiarize yourself with a multitude of marketing tactics. The approach that works best for you will depend on the product you are selling. Try everything, track the results and increase your focus on the marketing methods that work the best. Although this book will not cover marketing in depth, you may want to read Guerrilla Marketing Breakthrough Strategies for a bullet proof way to market your online business with little capital investment. http://www.TheGuerrillaGuys.com

Develop a Plan.

Without a blueprint for reaching your goals, you'll have a hard time focusing and difficulty hitting your target. Having a plan provides you with focus, direction and momentum to keep your business on track. We will look further at setting up a business plan shortly.

Check Laws and Regulations

It is important that you check to see if there are any local laws or regulations in relation to setting up an online business from home. Also, you will need to set up your business in accordance with the laws and regulations in your area.

Setting up your office

More often than not, an online business will be conducted from the person's home. So it is important that you set up a home office prior to starting up the business. You should arrange to have all the necessary equipment that you will need such as computer, Internet connection, and a printer.

How to Set Up Your Business Plan

By setting up a business plan, you have a road map to success. It will help you develop your business goals and strategies, as well as provide you with a better understanding of the marketplace. It will also highlight any business strengths or weaknesses you may have, and provide you with an opportunity to take a close look at your competitors. You can also include financial projections, historical data and growth expectations in your business plan.

With any good business plan, it should show who the target audience is, and how the product or service will meet or exceed their needs and expectations.

When organizing a business plan, break it down into sections such as:

- Business summary – The product or service you will provide.

- Market analysis – Research on the product or service and how the competitors are doing.

- Product positioning – How to make it more prominent compared to your competitors.

- Market strategy – How are you actually going to market it?

- Customer analysis – Look at what the customer wants or needs.

- Financial analysis – What you need to invest in order to set up the business and keep it going while it is just getting started.

- Overall business goals – What you hope to achieve in one, two and five years.

Once a business plan has been developed, it should not lay in the back of a drawer somewhere. It should be a working plan that you can refer to when you need to.

The best way to make a business plan is to keep it simple (one or two pages should be all you need).

Certainly one of the best things you can do when starting an online business is to create a plan and stick with it.

What Type of Business Is Best For You?

In this chapter, we will look at some of the more common types of online businesses that people are running. Keep in mind, the decision is up to you as to what type of business you want to run.

Marketing Business

This is one of the most common types of online businesses. You can either run this business by exclusively marketing your own products, or by marketing those from other companies. In order for this business to be successful, it needs to be promoted effectively to potential customers via search engines, email or other sources. We will look at marketing in more depth later in this book.

Turnkey Internet Business

This is a very trendy type of business. You purchase a website and then run the business on a web platform that is provided by the business. In order to promote such an online business, there are many different methods you could use, such as promoting individual products or services to your online customers.

Internet Services

This is a business where specific services are provided to online customers. Many times, these businesses are set up according to a person's professional expertise. The types of businesses under this umbrella are online consulting, computer software assistance, hardware trouble shooting and even how to start an online business.

In addition to the ones mentioned above, there are many other kinds of online businesses too. You've got entertainment websites, interior design, dating, article writing, fitness, medical, online chat and the list is endless. It doesn't really matter what kind of online business ("niche") you decide to get involved in, it is important to plan carefully and have the ability promote the business professionally over the Internet. The only limit is your imagination.

How to Set Up an Online Business

Here is the recipe for setting up your online business:

- Choose a niche and specialize in it.

- Choose or create a product. You can either use affiliate products or create your own.

- Choose a good business name. It should be short, easy to remember and reflect what your business actually does. Your domain name is what your customers will remember you by. A good domain name is one that is memorable, short and easy to spell. I recommend registering your domain with http://www.NameCheap.com

- Hosting. Always look for a secure and reliable hosting service. It is important that you examine the "uptime guarantee" that each service provider offers. Also, analyze the physical infrastructure of where your online business will be stored. But probably most important of all is that you should scrutinize the hosting providers "Back Up" and "Data Security" systems. This includes calculating how much time would be required to reinstall your online business if there was a complete infrastructure failure on the part of the hosting provider. This will help you to calculate the least possible loss to your business. I recommend http://www.HostGator.com

- Set up a professional looking website. You can get free website templates from http://www.oswd.org or hire a web design company like http://www.iClickGraphicsClub.com You don't need to be super technical to do this.

- Build a list of subscribers. This is important so you can follow up with visitors to your site. It is important that you keep the visitors updated as to what is happening with your site. This also enables you to contact them numerous times regarding your offers.

- Payments. If you are selling an affiliate product, this will not be an issue, as the affiliate program will handle the payments for you. However, if you are selling your own product, you will have to set up your own payment processing system. This can be done easily using a payment processor like: http://www.PayPal.com http://www.2CheckOut.com http://www.ClickBank.com

- Delivery. If you're selling tangible products, you'll want to contact local courier companies, as well as the postal service and find out which will be more cost effective for shipping your products. Also, you will need to set up your shipping fee structure. It is important that you choose a shipping company who you know is reliable. Look for a company who offer an online tracking system.

Affiliate Marketing Explained

Affiliate Marketing is basically commission sales. As an affiliate, you are paid a commission based on the sales you generate. You may also be paid for your referrals completing a specific action, like signing up for a newsletter.

Many companies like to use affiliate marketing because they do not incur any marketing expenses unless the desired results are achieved.

There are a multitude of benefits for being an affiliate:

No Production Costs

With an affiliate program, production costs are not an issue as the product has already been produced.

Little Capital Investment

All you will need is a computer with an Internet connection and a website. Assuming you already have a computer, you can start your affiliate business for less than $20.

Choices

There are thousands of products and services that you can choose from. Browse through

http://www.ClickBank.com

http://www.CommissionJunction.com

You'll probably find more affiliate programs to join than you could ever possibly promote, so choose wisely and prosper :)

No Merchant Account

This can be a time consuming and costly expense for anyone setting up a business for the first time. However, as an affiliate, the merchant you are selling the product for will bear all the sales costs. So you never have to worry about any potential charge backs, fraudulent purchases or losing your merchant account completely.

No Customer Service

You don't have to worry about dealing with awkward or nasty customers and their complaints. This is the merchant's responsibility.

Quick Change

If the first product you chose to market isn't making money, you can just dump it. Remove any links to the product and then start promoting a different product.

If you work hard at affiliate marketing, you can earn a good income. Some top affiliates earn high 6 and 7 figure incomes.

Online Payment Systems

There are many online payment services which provide you with a simple way to accept payments. Unlike banks and credit card companies, services such as PayPal and

ClickBank don't require a business to have a merchant account. They process the orders for you and the money is transferred to your bank account electronically.

Such services have become especially popular among those who use online auction sites (such as Ebay), but many other online businesses are beginning to see the advantages of these services as well.

Although these services charge a small processing fee, it's less than you would normally pay for a credit card merchant account. Also, such services can be especially helpful when you need to arrange for small repetitive payments for hosting or an autoresponder.

But there are some drawbacks to using a payment service.

1. Many of them impose a daily or weekly limit on the amount of money that you send or receive. So if you want to exceed these limits you may find yourself incurring an additional fee for a "business account" or "premiere account".

2. These services are not banks, and therefore are not subject to strict banking regulations or protected by Federal Deposit Insurance.

3. Often these services provide their customers with less protection against fraud and abuse than many credit card companies offer.

4. Also, they are sometimes quick to freeze a customer's account if they suspect fraudulent or other criminal activities are taking place.

Before you sign up to any payment service, read their terms and conditions thoroughly. It is important that you fully understand and accept the service's dispute policy, limits on liability, their fee structure and any other rules or regulations that they may have.   It is also important that you do not keep too much money in your account, rather keep enough to conduct a few days of business and any unused funds should be transferred over to your regular bank account.

Following are a few more payment services that you may want to look at further when setting up an online business account.

- Authorize.net. This service processes credit card and checking account transactions.

- BidPay. This allows person to person payments. They accept a credit card payment from the payer and then send a money order to the payee.

- BillPoint. This also allows person to person payments. Originally this system was being targeted specifically at Ebay customers.

- E-Gold. This allows the payment in gold (silver, platinum or palladium) to be made from one customer to another using an account based system.

- PayPal. This is probably the most well known payment service. It allows user to user payments and money transfers from funds in the user's PayPal account. It also allows payments by credit card and eCheck.

- World Pay. This service provides both an Internet merchant account, and payment processing service in one package.

How To Marketing Your Online Business

The first thing you need to do is learn how to optimize your website so that it will start getting ranked in the search engines. The most important search engine is Google, followed by Yahoo, MSN and Bing. The sooner you do this, the faster it will get ranked and the sooner the traffic will start to appear.

Search Engine Optimization (SEO) is an entire industry with a multitude of ways to optimize your website. But the most important factor in SEO is the number of websites that are linked to yours.

Here are a few ways to get other webmasters to link to your website:

Link Exchanges

You exchange links with other websites that have complimentary products or services to your own. It will give you direct traffic from the link and help you rank higher in the search engines.

Write Articles

It is important that the articles you write are interesting and full of useful information regarding your niche. This is probably one of the best ways to gain more traffic to your website.

Not only is it free, but when you post your article on article directories, you will be providing a link back to your site which helps get you a better ranking in the search engines and traffic.

However, if you are someone who dislikes writing, you could always use a ghostwriter. There are many sites offering ghostwriting services or freelancers who will write for you. Check out:

http://www.eLance.com

http://www.Guru.com

Online Forums

When you post on an online forum, include your signature at the end of any comments you make. This will provide a further link back to your site and get click-throughs from the forum participants.

Your signature file includes your name, a small blurb about you or your product and a link to your website.

Participating in forums also helps you learn about your potential customer's desires, and establish yourself as an expert in the field.

Blogs

Blogs are a great way of ensuring you get back links to your site. But ensure that you post to your blog several times a week and think of it as a news page for your site. Certainly blogging has become the "in" thing at the moment on the web.

Conclusion

An online business allows you the freedom to start up with almost no capital . You don't need an office, you can work from home, and you don't need employees. Your main expenses are a computer and an Internet connection.

However, the most important aspect of any online business is to generate traffic to your site. So get a strategy in place which will generate the traffic required to bring in those all important visitors, which convert into sales.

Good luck with your future online ventures!

Bonus

Get Related Materials

from Our Free Library

Instant Access – Join Here

Click or type into your browser:

http://livesensical.com/go/byob/

www.ingramcontent.com/pod-product-compliance
Lightning Source LLC
Chambersburg PA
CBHW021857170526
45157CB00006B/2488

* 9 7 8 1 3 2 9 9 6 7 0 9 0 *